START-UP ▲
ROCK GUITAR
It's never been easier to start playing rock guitar!

Published by
Wise Publications
14-15 Berners Street, London W1T 3LJ, UK.

Exclusive Distributors:
Music Sales Limited
Distribution Centre, Newmarket Road, Bury St Edmunds, Suffolk IP33 3YB, UK.
Music Sales Pty Limited
20 Resolution Drive, Caringbah, NSW 2229, Australia.

Order No. AM1002925
ISBN: 978-1-84938-983-9
This book © Copyright 2011 Wise Publications, a division of Music Sales Limited.

Adapted by David Harrison from an original book by Artie Traum.
Produced by shedwork.com
Design by Fresh Lemon.
Photography by Matthew Ward.
Model: Sagat Guirey.
Edited by Tom Farncombe.
Printed in the EU

With thanks to the City Lit, London.

Your Guarantee of Quality
As publishers, we strive to produce every book to the highest commercial standards.
This book has been carefully designed to minimise awkward page turns and to make playing
from it a real pleasure. Particular care has been given to specifying acid-free, neutral-sized
paper made from pulps which have not been elemental chlorine bleached. This pulp is from
farmed sustainable forests and was produced with special regard for the environment.
Throughout, the printing and binding have been planned to ensure a sturdy, attractive
publication which should give years of enjoyment. If your copy fails to meet our high standards,
please inform us and we will gladly replace it.

www.musicsales.com

WISE PUBLICATIONS
part of The Music Sales Group
London / New York / Paris / Sydney / Copenhagen / Berlin / Madrid / Hong Kong / Tokyo

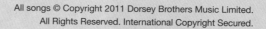

From Chuck Berry to the Beatles, Led Zeppelin to Oasis, AC/DC to Radiohead, new styles and innovations have continued to revolutionise rock guitar playing since its early days in the 1950s, when disc jockey Alan Freed first coined the phrase 'rock 'n' roll'.

Thousands—perhaps millions—of guitar fans have struggled on their electric guitars since then, shattering their neighbours' eardrums while trying to recreate the sounds they've heard.

For some, playing the guitar leads to fame and fortune. But most people strum at home for personal enjoyment, unravelling the mysteries of the guitar at their own pace.

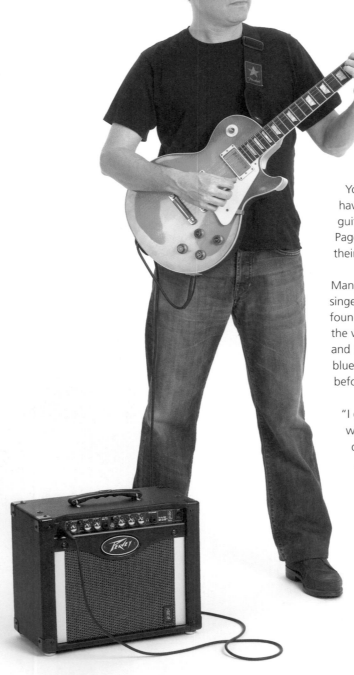

In the early days, a sense of tradition tied rock guitarists to the blues of the past—particularly the urban blues from Chicago, Memphis, Detroit and New Orleans. Players like B.B. King, Elmore James and Albert King had a powerful influence on the rock players of the time. Indeed most rock guitarists still rely on a blues-based vocabulary, including string bending, shuffle licks, and 'blue' notes played against major chords.

Of course, things have come a long way since then. But as New Orleans guitarist Clarence 'Gatemouth' Brown says, "All American popular music derives from the blues. You simply can't play rock 'n' roll or jazz unless you have a solid blues foundation..." Indeed, all rock guitarists worth their salt—from Eric Clapton to Jimmy Page, from Carlos Santana to Joe Satriani—have noted their debt to the blues.

Many rock guitarists began by playing back-up to singers. People like Scotty Moore and James Burton found themselves tossing-in licks and riffs to embellish the vocals of performers like Elvis Presley, Rick Nelson, and Buddy Holly. These musicians learned their 12-bar blues styles first, as well as various country music styles, before branching out into uncharted territory.

"I got an early introduction to rhythm and blues music when I was just 16," Pete Townshend of The Who once said. "I was into stuff like John Lee Hooker, Jimmy Reid and B.B. King before anyone else..." Many rock players, including the Rolling Stones, Clapton and Hendrix, were under the spell of urban blues for years before breaking out into their own dynamic styles. We will begin our study of rock 'n' roll guitar in the same manner—with the blues, a touch of country music, and some basic chords.

The guitar is an incredibly versatile instrument and the sounds, effects and melodies that emerge from it constantly amaze. Still, one has to start at the beginning. Where else?

Jimmy Page, leader of Led Zeppelin, said he "started out very slowly" with an old steel-string Spanish guitar that his parents had in the house. "I went to guitar shops, watching what people were doing, trying to learn. In the end it was the other way, and people were watching me."

Page, however, had no patience for guitar lessons. He made his own way on the instrument by "spending hours trying to figure out" the riffs and chords on recordings he loved. "The first ones were Buddy Holly chord solos," he revealed in an interview in Tobler and Grundy's *The Guitar Greats*. "... songs like 'Peggy Sue'. The next step was definitely James Burton [the lead guitarist on Ricky Nelson's records]. It was the bending strings style that really got me going."

Of course, instruction books can give you many helpful hints and point you in the right direction. Books can show you notes, chords, and strumming ideas, but it's up to you to put grace and feeling into your playing.

As Ry Cooder once said: "you have to learn where it's coming from... that's the important part." Many guitarists have learned their craft by watching the people they respect and admire, listening closely to their recordings, and taking lessons.

Collect recordings that show different rock guitar styles and study them closely. Get as close as you can to the front at concerts to watch the lead and rhythm guitarists' hands. Exchange licks and riffs with friends.

Most important, however, is to stick with it. Don't give up. Guitar playing, particularly good rock 'n' roll, takes long hours of practice and dedication. Still, it should be fun for you!

Rock 'n' roll took the post-war blues singing style and set it against the rhythm with repetitive chords on piano or guitar... the effect was overpowering

Samuel Charters, blues historian

I'd have been locked up long ago if I hadn't had a guitar...

Jeff Beck

A WORD ON EQUIPMENT

Rock guitarists love equipment. There are seemingly endless options for amplifiers and effects pedals to plug your guitar into. However, to get to grips with the basics of playing guitar, it's best to start simple.

The material in this book, in fact, could be played on a simple acoustic guitar—although an electric guitar plugged into a small amplifier is probably the best set-up. In general, electric guitars are easier to play than acoustics.

The lighter strings on a typical electric make it easier to finger chord shapes, since the strings are lighter.

But, at this point, it's not absolutely necessary to go electric.

Whatever guitar you choose, there are a few pointers that will make your playing more fun. First of all, your instrument should have a straight neck, easy action, and some light-gauge strings (0.09 – 0.42).

A solid-body guitar will give more bite to your sound, while hollow-bodied guitars will sound somewhat mellow. Hollow-body guitars were originally acoustic guitars with electric pickups mounted in them to produce a jazzy, rounded tone. Since they feedback more easily at high volume levels, they can cause problems if you wish to play very loudly.

It's very tempting to go straight for one of the classic rock guitars, like the Fender Stratocaster or Telecaster, or the Gibson Les Paul or SG. But at this point, don't let your ego decide which guitar to buy. There are some great bargains out there and for now, you should settle for the best buy for your budget. There is no point in breaking the bank.

A hollow-bodied guitar, like this Gibson 335-style Heritage, is a great choice for the mellower end of rock, and if feedback's what you're after, it might be just the thing for you!

Amplifiers

To start with, it's best to select a small practice amp—between 5watts and 20watts—that you can get a good sound with while practising at home.

Initially, set the amp's tone controls about halfway and keep the gain and volume controls low to get an even, crisp sound.

Holding the Guitar

Although this might seem straightforward, it's easy to develop bad habits from the outset if you don't take a few simple precautions.

These habits can lead to serious muscle pains and problems with posture, and can seriously limit your technique, so it's worth taking a moment to look closely at your hand and body position.

If you're sitting, find a straight-backed chair (without arms) to sit on, and hold the guitar on your lap. Alternatively, a stool that allows you to support your feet on a rail is a good choice (right). Once you're seated comfortably, you will be looking down at the guitar from the bird's-eye view. You'll probably find a strap will help to hold the guitar in place. If you choose to stand, a strap is an absolute must. Again you'll be looking straight down on the guitar and you'll see precious little of the fingerboard and strings.

Get used to feeling for position: constantly looking down and lifting the guitar up towards you will hamper your progress. Many beginners sit or stand in front of a mirror to check what their hands are doing and these days, a web cam can easily be used instead.

The left hand, especially, will need all the help it can get! Try to keep your shoulders relaxed, your wrists and elbows nice and loose and, if you're standing, keep your weight evenly spread on both legs.

TUNING

Getting the guitar in tune is a crucial skill. There are various methods, but they all involve adjusting the pitch of the open (unfretted) strings by turning the tuning pegs to tighten or loosen each string until it sounds the correct note. Let's look at the main methods.

Tuning the thicker strings can pull on the guitar neck enough to affect all the other strings, so there's no point in carefully tuning the thinner strings only to have to retune them once you've tuned the thicker ones.

Let's look at the sound source method first. These diagrams show the notes you need on the piano, the equivalent musical notation, and the appropriate strings on the guitar.

Notice how the strings are named (above right): the bottom string is the one that sounds lowest. The top string is the highest-sounding.

You can choose a sound source to tune against, such as a piano, pitch pipes, special audio tracks or a tuning fork; or else you can use an electronic tuner, which will tell you when your guitar is in tune.

Either way, you should start with the thickest (also known as the *bottom*, or *sixth*) string, and work your way through the strings to the thinnest (*top*, or *first*).

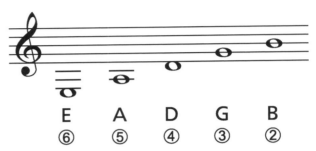

E   A   D   G   B
⑥   ⑤   ④   ③   ②

By the way: in guitar notation, notes are written an octave higher than the actual sounding pitch.

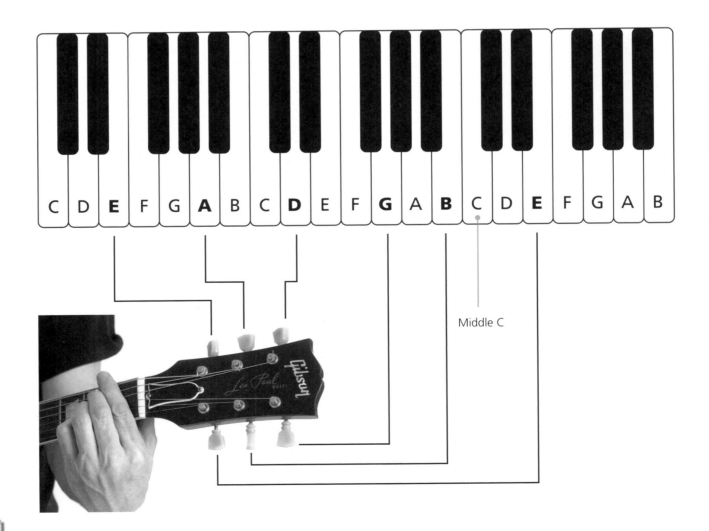

Middle C

Relative Tuning

If you tune the bottom string accurately, you can then use that string to tune the others.

Here's how it works:

- Place a finger on the 5th fret of the bottom (sixth) string—this will give you the note you need (A) to tune the open fifth string.

- Once that's done, play a note on the 5th fret of the fifth string. It'll be D, which is the note you need for the open fourth string.

- And again, play a note on the 5th fret of the fourth string to give you the note you need (G) for the open third string.

- Now the sequence changes: this time, play a note on the 4th fret of the third string to sound B, which is the correct note for the open second string.

- Finally, play a note on the 5th fret of the second string to sound E, which is the note you'll need to tune the top string.

Although it might seem a bit fiddly, this method is great for checking a single string if you're in the middle of playing, and since it relies on your ears it's great training too... check the diagram below for fret positions for each of the reference notes.

Clip-on style tuners are especially convenient (see the section on electronic tuners, below).

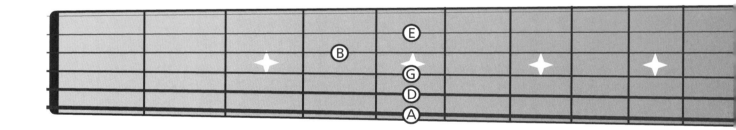

Electronic Tuners

Using an electronic tuner has lots of advantages: they're pretty fool-proof, and very precise.

And, if you're tuning in a noisy situation, plugging a tuner in or attaching it to the guitar means you can tune even if you can't hear the guitar properly.

Play the bottom string, and the device will show you on its display whether you're low or high.

Tune the string in the right direction and, when it's up to pitch, the display will let you know. Simply move on to the next string and so on, until the instrument is tuned.

CHORDS: THE FOUNDATION OF ROCK 'N' ROLL

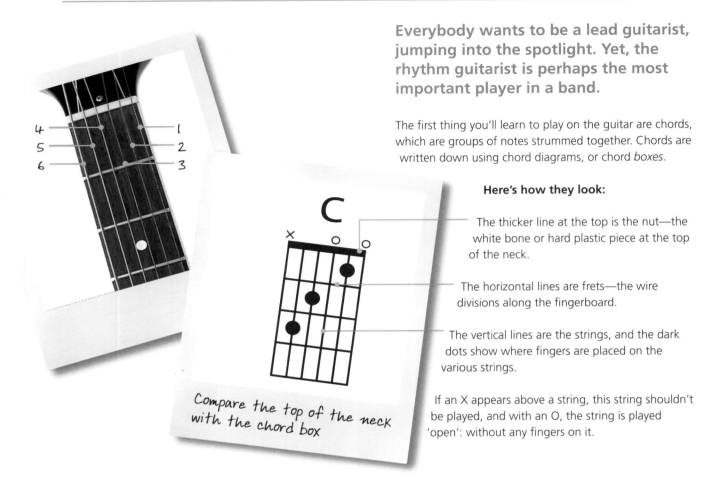

Compare the top of the neck with the chord box

Everybody wants to be a lead guitarist, jumping into the spotlight. Yet, the rhythm guitarist is perhaps the most important player in a band.

The first thing you'll learn to play on the guitar are chords, which are groups of notes strummed together. Chords are written down using chord diagrams, or chord *boxes*.

Here's how they look:

The thicker line at the top is the nut—the white bone or hard plastic piece at the top of the neck.

The horizontal lines are frets—the wire divisions along the fingerboard.

The vertical lines are the strings, and the dark dots show where fingers are placed on the various strings.

If an X appears above a string, this string shouldn't be played, and with an O, the string is played 'open': without any fingers on it.

The strings are numbered 1-6, starting with the thinnest (or 'top') string, down to the thickest (or 'bottom') string (above).

Left-hand fingers are numbered 1-4 from the index finger to the little finger (below).

Here's how the chord boxes are used in this book—they are displayed upright, accompanied by a photograph of the fingers in a natural, horizontal position. Compare the diagram below with the photograph to see how they relate to one another.

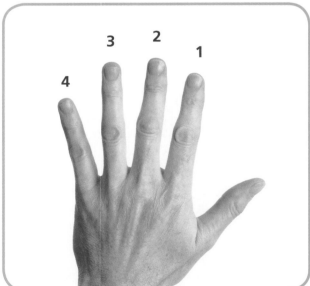

Let's start with an E chord—one that you'll use time and again in rock 'n' roll. It looks like this:

Make sure you do this correctly. Your 1st finger presses the third string at the 1st fret; your 2nd finger presses the fifth string at the 2nd fret; and your 3rd finger presses the fourth string at the 2nd fret.

You must push down with enough strength to make the notes clearly sound, taking care that your other fingers don't block the open strings. In other words, arch your hands around the neck so that the notes ring out clearly. Strum down across the strings with your right hand and you should hear an E chord.

For now, curl the fingers of your right hand slightly as you strum with your fingernails. Later on, we'll get into using a pick.

You'll notice that your left fingertips will start to become sore as you play these first chords. Don't worry about it: no pain, no gain. The soreness is only temporary—it will go away. After a while, you will develop calluses that will protect your fingers when playing.

Left hander?

If you happen to be left handed, there's nothing standing in your way to playing the guitar. There are plenty of left handed guitars out there, and as you work through this book, you'll simply need to reverse everything you see.

Okay, let's get back to chords. Do you understand the E chord? Now, let's go on to the A chord. It looks like this:

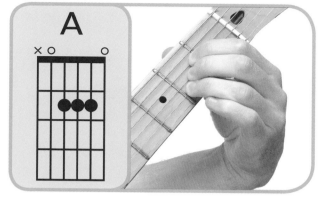

Line your fingers up for the chord. Now strum across again, this time being careful to avoid the bottom string.

If you're having trouble with the chords, press your thumb gently onto the back of the guitar neck as shown in this photo. This will add the extra leverage you need.

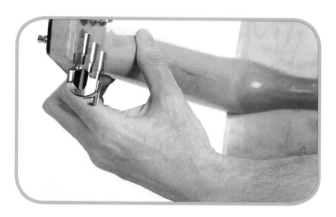

Make sure that your fingers are pressing the strings very close to the fret, without actually being on the fret itself. You don't have to strain to push down, but make sure you're exerting enough pressure so that the notes ring clearly.

Now try going back and forth from the E chord to the A chord (slowly at first) with four beats to each chord, like this:

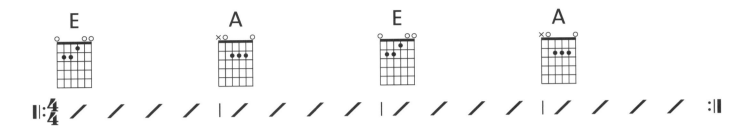

The secret of playing guitar well is your ability to change chords at will. Each slash in the example above gets one strum with your right hand. Four slashes make up one *bar*, or measure of music. As you change chords, check how smooth your strumming is. It should be easy and effortless.

Let's try one more chord, B7. When you have learned this one additional chord, you will have all the chords you need to play hundreds of songs in the key of E.

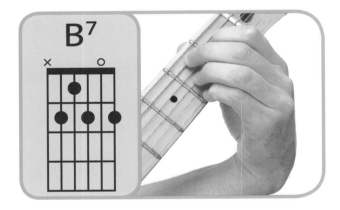

One point to mention: when you play the A and B7 chords, stay away from the low E string while strumming. Notice in both diagrams the 'x' above the 6th string, indicating that the string should not be played.

It'll take a bit of practice before you can reliably strum across the strings without making contact with the bottom string, and you shouldn't be too concerned for now. You'll soon begin to develop a sense of where the strings are and how to strum only certain ones.

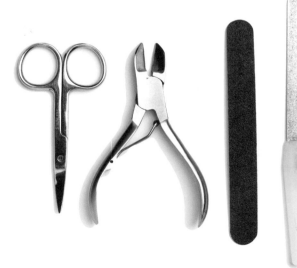

Keep the nails on your left hand short so they don't dig into the fingerboard. Your right-hand nails may stay long if you wish—particularly if you intend to play finger style guitar at some point.

The exercise opposite and the piece on this page are repeated. This is indicated by the repeat marks. Music appearing within these marks is played twice:

Strum each chord on the beat. As with the previous exercise, keep a steady rhythm; change smoothly from one chord to another; and try to use as little force as possible. The music should flow freely.

12-BAR BLUES IN E

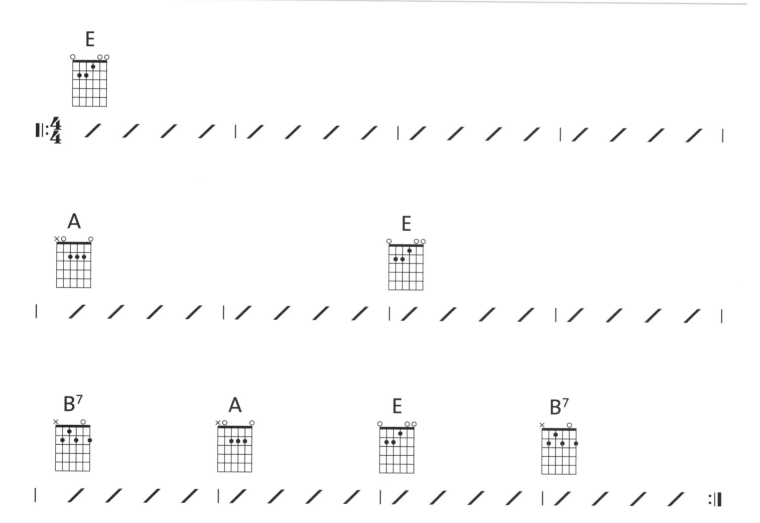

There are literally hundreds of blues songs that can be played with these chords. Once you have mastered the chords, you can try out other songs on your own. Take a look at an example overleaf.

GOOD MORNIN' BLUES

We are getting into some relatively new territory here, but we want to get playing as soon as possible. Keep practising these chord changes until you can play them smoothly. Once you can, you'll be able to play the first song with these chords, a popular early blues called 'Good Mornin' Blues'.

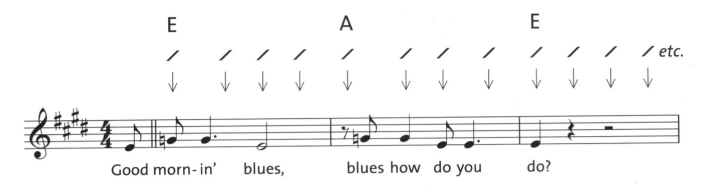

Good morn-in' blues, blues how do you do?

Good morn-in' blues, blues how do you

do? Well I'm do-in' all right,_ good

morn-in' how are you?

Don't worry if you can't read music; just strum the chords and sing along. If you don't know the tunes in this book, check out some recordings. 'Good Mornin' Blues' exists in many versions, such as those by Leadbelly and Davy Graham.

A WORD ABOUT PRACTISING

There is so much to learn, so much to absorb, and so much to consider in music that it's important to be discriminating. You should pick and choose what's important to you, and studiously go about learning it.

After a while, it will become part of your memory and you'll be able to play without even thinking about it.

The secret to this is in continually repeating some of the key tasks, such as changing chords smoothly, strumming in time and memorising chord sequences.

As a beginner, however, you will be faced with the 'frustration factor', when a riff, chord or song stays just outside of your grasp for a while. Simply forget it. After a time, come back to it. It's funny sometimes how some things click for musicians. Just when you think you'll never get the knack of something, it suddenly becomes clear—and easy!

Here are a few tips to help you progress by making the best use of your practice time:

- A little practice every day is much more valuable than a finger-numbing mammoth session once a week.

- Keep a check on your posture and technique, to avoid any niggles creeping into your playing.

- Start slowly and build up: there will be a little wear and tear on your fingers to begin with, and it will take a bit of time to build up the calluses on your left fingertips—it's easy to overdo it, especially at the beginning.

- Set a target for each practice session, and make it realistic. Some people keep a practice diary, making a note of things to try in the next session. It's a great way to record your progress.

- Set aside time to play for fun. Keep it separate from your practice time, but make sure you sit and strum once in a while for no particular reason: after all, it's why you're learning to play guitar!

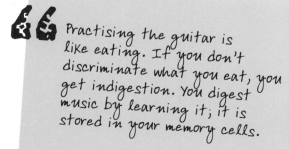

> Practising the guitar is like eating. If you don't discriminate what you eat, you get indigestion. You digest music by learning it; it is stored in your memory cells.
>
> Carlos Santana

SEVENTH CHORDS

The E7 and A7 chords will add some spice to your playing as you learn the blues progression.

They look like this, and can be used in place of the regular E or A chords:

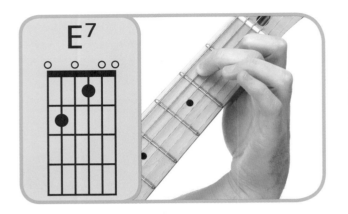 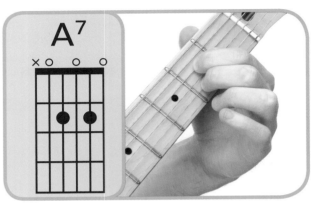

Let's try the 12-bar blues progression with the E7 and A7 chords alongside E, A and B7.

E   E7

A   A7   E7

B7   A7   E   B7

You can also try these alternate shapes—they can be played instead of the other shapes, and have a slightly different timbre:

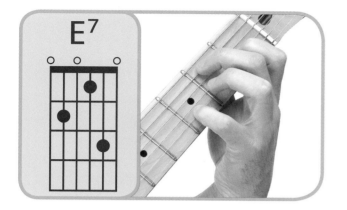

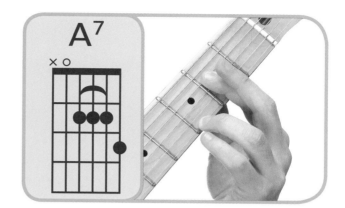

Hear how the addition of the seventh chords changes the musical texture in this next song.

See See Rider

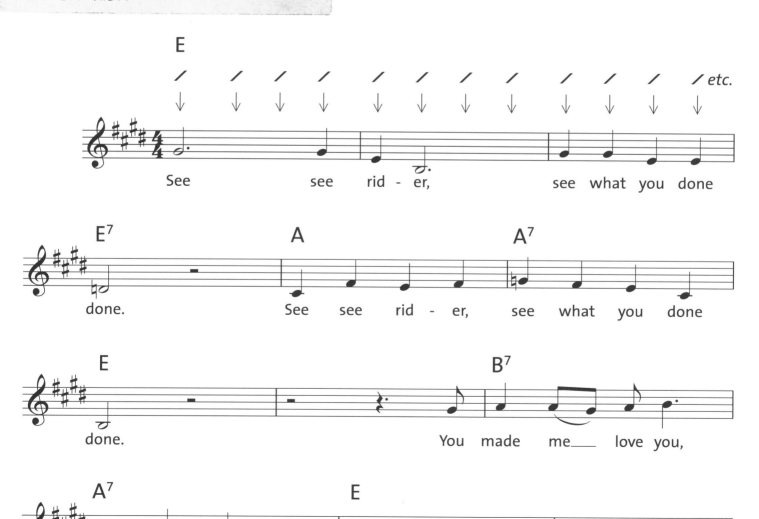

Let's take a look at groups of chords that you must learn in order to play rock 'n' roll. Take your time and learn each key separately.

As you will see, some chords overlap between keys. In the key of A, both the A and E chords appear—yet they are used in a different context than they were in the key of E. You'll see that chords generally appear in families of related shapes.

KEY OF A

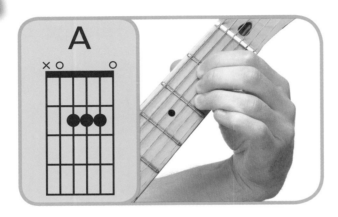

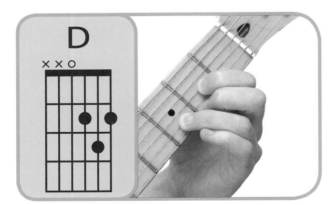

Get into the habit of learning chords as sets—the three chords on this page are the ones you're most likely to come across in the key of A. You'll find that E is often played as E7, but when you have a simple song in this key, these are the three chords you can expect to play.

In fact, if you've heard the expression 'three chord trick' it refers to a song using just these three chords.

Counting up (alphabetically) on the scale of A, you'll notice that A is the first note, whilst D is the fourth note and E the fifth note. In music, the chords that appear on the different steps of the scale are generally numbered using Roman numerals. Hence, these chords are **I**, **IV** and **V**.

In this section we're going to look at **I**, **IV** and **V** in various other common keys.

There are 100s of songs which you can play with A, D and E, such as 'Three Little Birds' by Bob Marley & The Wailers and 'Wild Thing' by The Troggs.

Now, you can play 'Good Mornin' Blues'
in the key of A. Transposed to A it
would look and sound like this:

Good Mornin' Blues

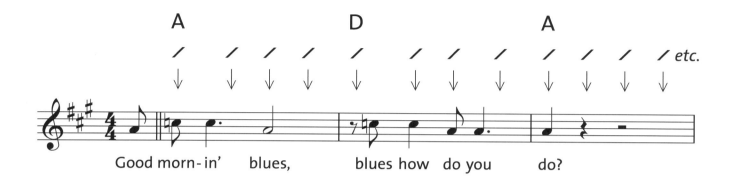

Good morn-in' blues,   blues how do you   do?

Good morn-in'   blues,   blues how   do   you

do?   Well I'm do-in' all   right,_ good

morn-in'   how are   you?

KEY OF D

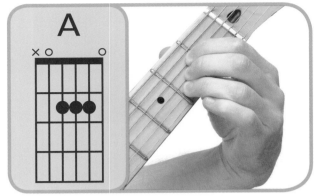

Likewise, here are **I**, **IV** and **V** in the key of D and, for completeness, here are the seventh versions for all three chords, too.

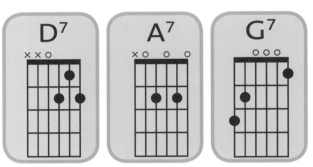

12-bar Blues in D

D			D⁷

D   D⁷

| 4/4 / / / / | / / / / | / / / / | / / / / |

G   G⁷   D⁷

| / / / / | / / / / | / / / / | / / / / |

A⁷   G⁷   D   A⁷

| / / / / | / / / / | / / / / | / / / / :‖

KEY OF G

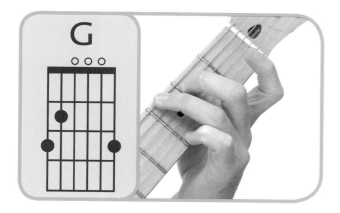

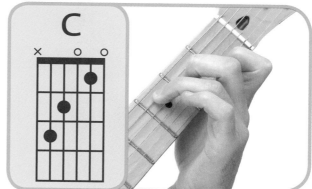

Same again for G this time, and again the optional sevenths which—in the blues at least—you can add to create a slightly different texture.

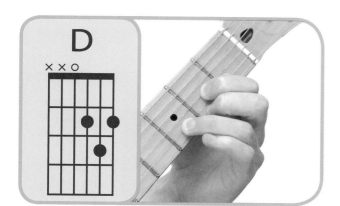

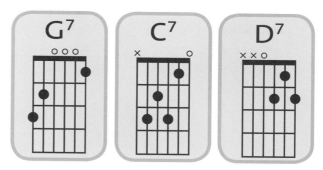

12-bar Blues in G

G			G⁷
$\frac{4}{4}$ ╱ ╱ ╱	╱ ╱ ╱	╱ ╱ ╱	╱ ╱ ╱

C	C⁷	G⁷	
╱ ╱ ╱	╱ ╱ ╱	╱ ╱ ╱	╱ ╱ ╱

D⁷	C⁷	G	D⁷
╱ ╱ ╱	╱ ╱ ╱	╱ ╱ ╱	╱ ╱ ╱ :||

KEY OF C

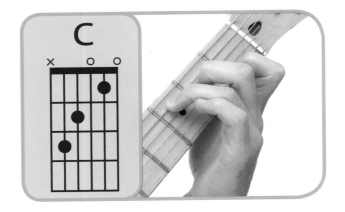

Finally, the equivalent seventh chords for the key of C. You'll notice the difference between the 4-string F and the 6-string F7. Check out the guide to bar chords (opposite) for more help.

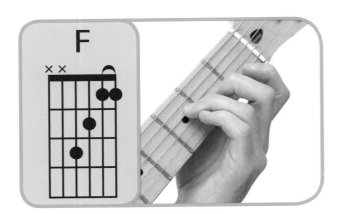

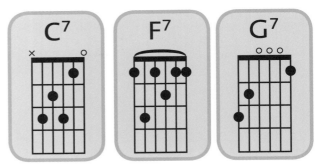

12-bar Blues in C

| C | | | | | C⁷ |

$\frac{4}{4}$ / / / / | / / / / | / / / / | / / / / |

| F | F⁷ | C | |

| / / / / | / / / / | / / / / | / / / / |

| G⁷ | F⁷ | C | G⁷ |

| / / / / | / / / / | / / / / | / / / / :||

BAR CHORDS EXPLAINED

Some of the shapes we've already looked at can be played higher up the neck as *bar chords*.

You'll notice that the F7 shape is formed by moving the E7 shape up one fret, with the addition of a finger that stretches right across all the strings on the 1st fret. The F7 shape is a bar chord (after *barre*, the classical guitar term for a finger that reaches over several strings at once).

You can use other E-type chord shapes, too. Create the basic shape and, using a bar, move it up the neck. Here, an E shape on the 7th fret makes B (below).

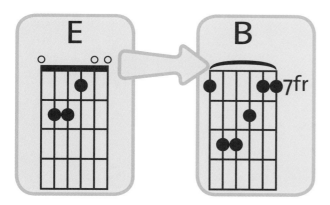

A-type chord shapes can also be used. An A shape barred on the 3rd fret makes a C chord (below left); and A minor barred on the 5th fret makes D minor (below right). Remember: with the E-type chord shapes, you'll need to

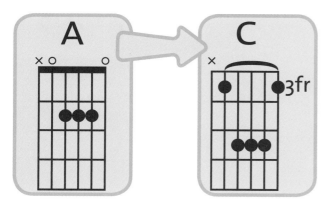

These are chords that use the first finger placed right across the fretboard, effectively shortening the neck for the duration of the chord. Compare these two chord shapes:

Every note of the E7 chord (including the open string notes) has been moved up one fret. So the chord is now one semitone higher—the distance from E to F. Practise putting the barre finger in place: it shouldn't need too much pressure, but might take some getting used to.

Try this new shape: it's a *minor* chord. In this example, an E minor shape is barred on the 3rd fret, making G minor (below).

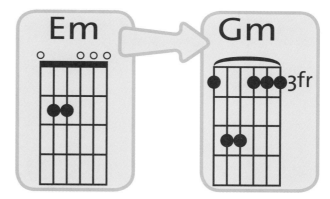

count up the sixth string to find the correct fret to bar. But for the A-type shapes, count up the fifth string. Take a look at the chart on page 48 to help orientate you on the neck for these chords.

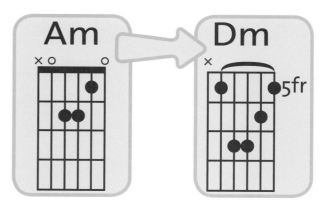

HOW TO READ TAB

There are several places on the guitar fretboard that you can play any particular note. This flexibility provides wonderful opportunities for varying tone, but it can be a headache for sight reading standard notation.

If you haven't yet learned to read either system, you should try learning tablature first. It's easier to learn, and it's mandatory for much guitar music, especially for alternate tunings. The music you'll play in the rest of this book will be written in both standard notation and tab. The tablature system consists of six horizontal lines, each representing a guitar string.

Tablature eliminates this problem. Tablature (or 'tab') is a musical notation system for stringed instruments that shows the performer exactly where to play each note on the fretboard.

This notation is used instead of (or alongside) standard notation, which shows the actual pitches.

The bass string is the bottom line of the tablature staff, and the treble string is the top line.

This layout is inverted from the actual string positions on the instrument. Here, the high-pitched notes lie high on the staff and the low-pitched notes lie low on the staff. In this way tablature resembles standard notation.

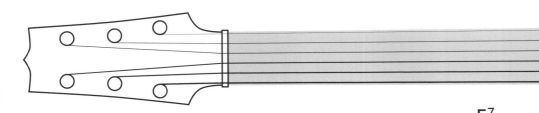

A number on a line indicates at which fret to depress that string.

This example (right) shows you where to fret the individual strings of an E7 shape, picked one string at a time.

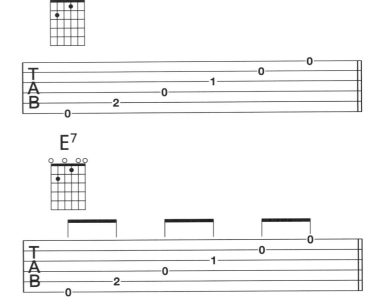

Sometimes, the stems and beams above or below the staff denote the rhythm. In the example here (right), the rhythm is a series of eighth notes.

Where two or more notes are played simultaneously, they are stacked up. Here's how a chord of E looks:

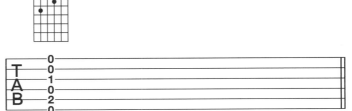

Rock guitarists like to use bends, slides, hammer-ons and various other embellishments in their playing. Here are some of the most common techniques, notated in tablature.

Semitone Bend

Strike the note and bend the string up a semitone (one fret's-worth in pitch). Many guitarists use two or even three left-hand fingers to help control the bend.

Whole tone Bend

Strike the note and bend the string up a tone (two frets'-worth in terms of pitch).

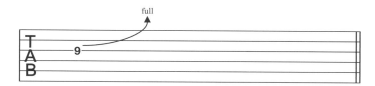

Bend and Release

Strike the note and bend the string up as indicated, then release back to the original note.

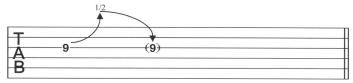

Compound Bend and Release

Strike the note and bend the string up and down as often as indicated.

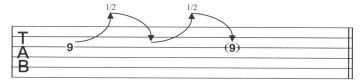

Pre-bend

Bend the string up the amount shown, then strike it.

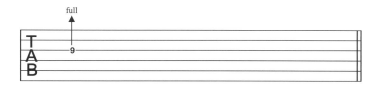

Pre-bend and Release

Bend the string up the amount shown, strike it and release back to the original pitch.

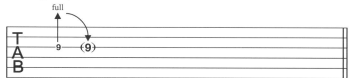

Hammer-on

Strike the first note, then bring a left-hand finger down onto the same string at the indicated fret without picking.

Pull-off

Place fingers on the indicated frets, then strike the string. Pull the higher finger off to sound the second note without picking.

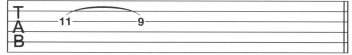

Legato Slide

Strike the first note, then move the fretting finger up or down to the next note without striking it.

Muffled Strings

Produce a percussive sound by laying your left-hand fingers loosely across the strings and picking them as normal.

THE SHUFFLE RIFF IN BLUES AND ROCK

In the early days of blues, guitarists like Robert Johnson accompanied their songs with a steady, thumping bass riff known as the 'shuffle riff'.

This kind of riff eventually became a major factor in rock 'n' roll guitar playing. You can hear examples of the style on songs like Chuck Berry's 'Memphis, Tennessee' and 'Johnny B. Goode', as well as many early Beatles songs.

Indeed, the shuffle riff travelled to England in the early 1960s, returning to the USA with the Rolling Stones,

In those days, many guitarists didn't work with drummers or bass players, so they needed a bass line moving with them.

the Dave Clark Five, the Yardbirds, and the Kinks—all of whom used the riff extensively. It is still used today, and will probably be with us for a long time to come.

This riff is very simple to play, although playing it well is another matter.

The first example of the shuffle riff is in the key of A, where it is easy to move from chord to chord. Essentially, you work with the fourth and fifth strings to play the riff on A.

You are only going to play two notes at a time. All other notes are dampened—that is, either muffled with the fingers of the left or right hand, or simply avoided. The 'x' at the top of the chord diagrams shows which notes to avoid. You'll need to pick carefully!

Place the 1st finger on the 2nd fret of the fourth string and pluck the fifth and fourth strings together with the thumb and 1st finger. Then place the 3rd finger onto the 4th fret of the fourth string, and pluck the pair of strings again.

Do this rhythmically, hitting each shape twice, as shown (see the note on *Swung Eighths*, opposite).

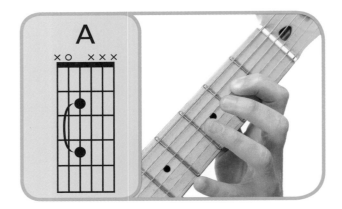

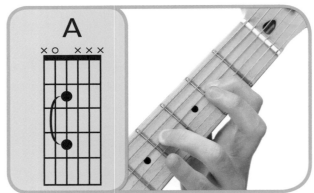

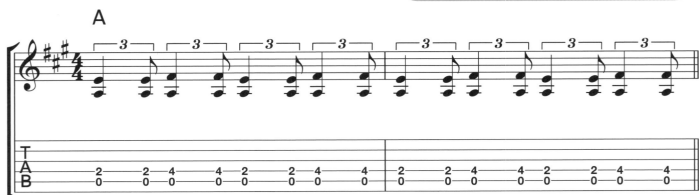

Swung Eighths

When pairs of eighth notes are swung, they are not played evenly. The first note is longer, and the second one shorter. In practice, this amounts to splitting the beat into thirds, with the first note of the pair lasting for two thirds of the beat and the second note lasting just the remaining third.

You'll notice that the exercises on these pages use triplets (beats divided into three), as shown by the square brackets above the pairs of notes.

Usually a metronome marking will show swung eighths.

Now try the same exercise, but with everything moved over to the fourth and third strings, making a riff in D instead.

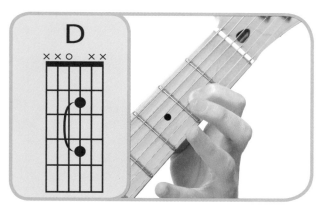

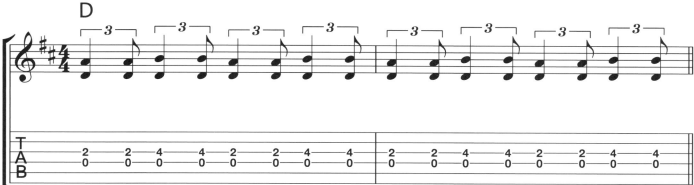

And finally, here it is in E, with the riff moved over to the bottom two strings:

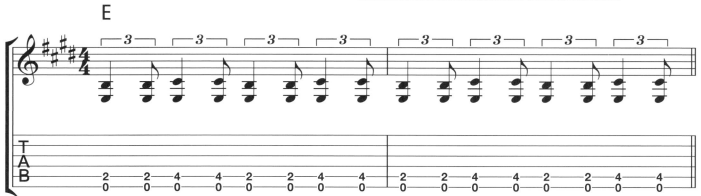

Now let's try the shuffle riff all the way through a 12-bar blues in the key of A.

Notice the metronome marking showing that eighth notes should be played with the same swung feel discussed on page 27.

12-bar Shuffle Blues in A

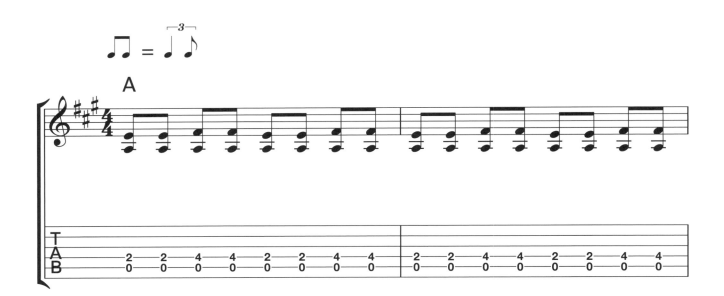

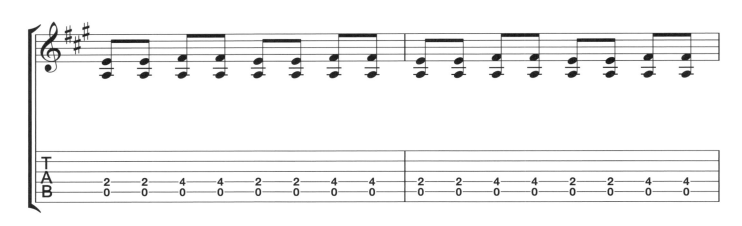

You'll need to practise changing between each riff; the shift from D to E might take a little work to make it sound clean.

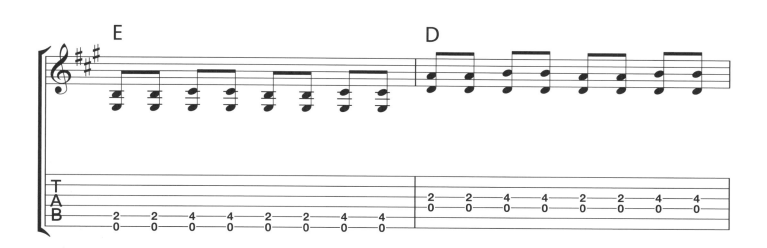

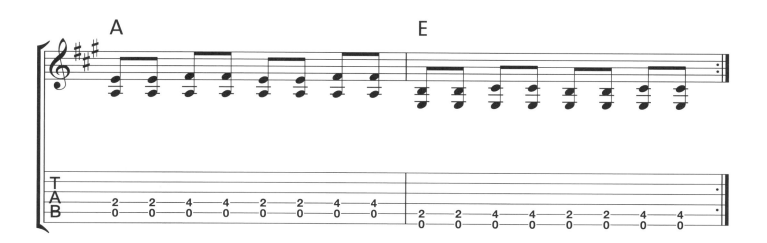

USING A PICK

Up to this point, we have been strumming and plucking with our fingers. Most rock guitarists however, use a flatpick (also known as a *plectrum*).

Picks come in three gauges—soft, medium, and hard. They're not expensive, so start by buying a few different ones and experimenting with them. The pick will feel bulky, awkward, and unruly at first—but after a while, you will get used to it. It will eventually become an extension of your right hand.

You'll find that different gauges of pick produce a different tone. And, as thin picks are more flexible and hard picks are stiffer, you might prefer different picks for different techniques. It's simply a matter of personal choice.

Hold the pick between your right thumb and index finger: not too tight, but not too loose either.

As in most aspects of guitar playing, you need to exert a fair amount of pressure without overdoing it. Keep this in mind as you strum or hit single notes with the pick. The most distinctive quality of any good guitarist is his or her touch. Never mind whether someone can play 100 notes a second. If you can play one note well—with grace, dignity and feeling—then you've already proved yourself as a musician.

Midnight Special is one of the most popular blues songs of all time, and it suits the shuffle riff perfectly. Keep in mind that the song begins on a D chord—even though it is in the key of A.

Try using a pick rather than your fingers to strum through this song. If you want to hear how it could sound, check

out the versions by Van Morrison, Little Richard and Leadbelly among others.

With a pick, you might find it easiest to strum down on every chord. Have a go at strumming *up* on the short off-beat notes, too. It might make the music flow a little more easily.

Midnight Special

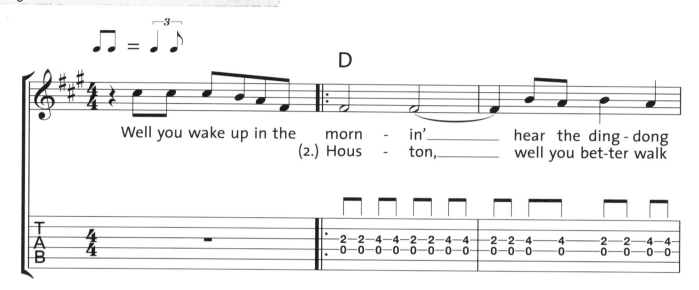

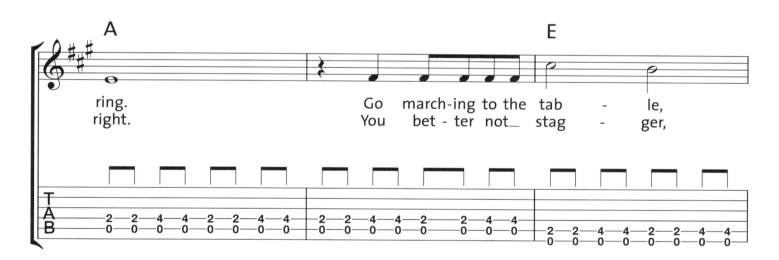

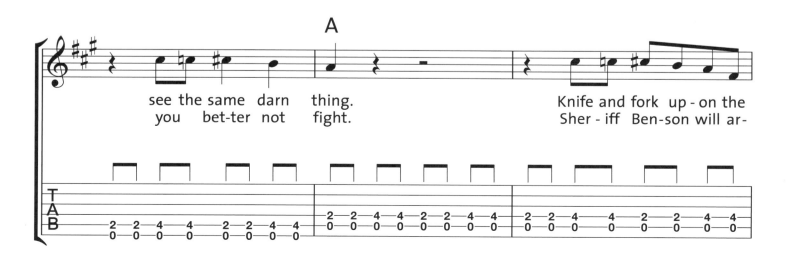

tab - le, noth-in' in my pan.
- rest you, he will car-ry you down.

And if you say a thing a - bout it,
And if the ju - ry finds you guilt - - y,

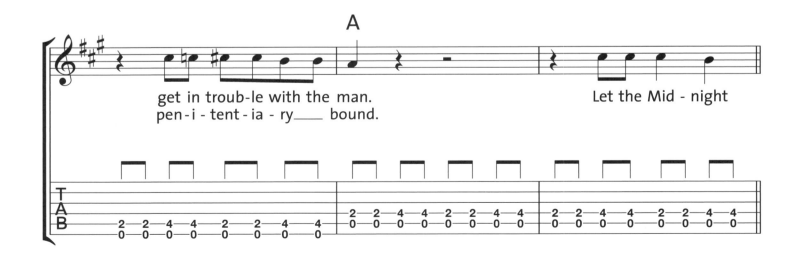

get in troub-le with the man.
pen - i - tent - ia - ry____ bound.

Let the Mid - night

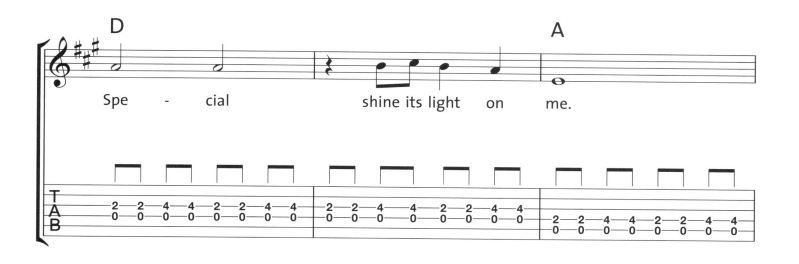

Spe - cial   shine its light   on   me.

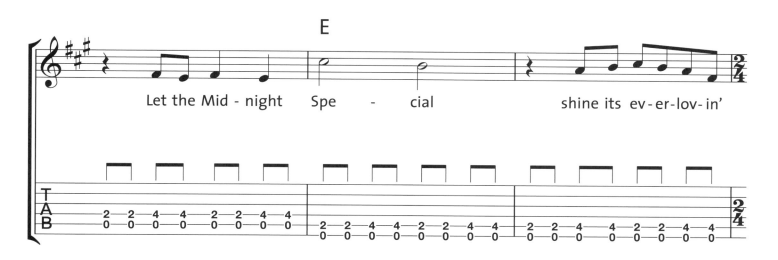

Let the Mid - night   Spe - cial   shine its ev-er-lov-in'

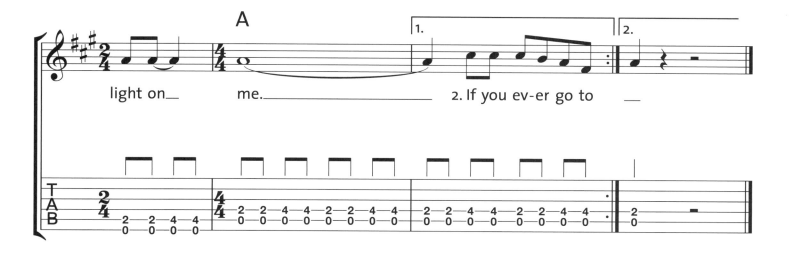

light on__   me._____   2. If you ev-er go to __

SHUFFLE RIFF VARIATION

By adding one more note to the shuffle riff, we can obtain a much more interesting sound.

Listen to different versions of 'Memphis, Tennessee' by Chuck Berry to hear how rock's greatest guitarists have used this variation.

This time, aside from the notes on the 2nd and 4th frets, there's an additional note on the 5th fret. This is played with the little finger, as shown in the photo.

Keep your thumb well-positioned at the back of the neck to balance your hand and ensure that you can apply even, controlled pressure with your fingertips.

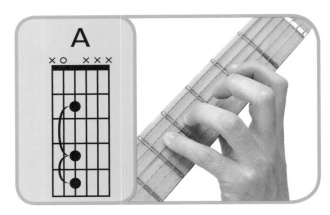

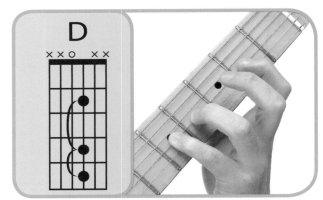

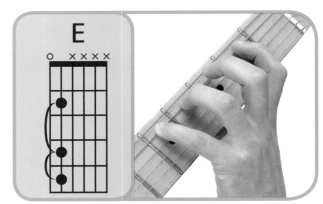

Here's how the riff looks in tab. Once you can play it smoothly in all three positions, try playing a 12-bar blues sequence as before.

As for picking, alternate up and down—but make sure you're always strumming down at the start of the beat.

This means that the three notes together on the last beat of the bar will throw you out of sync, so watch out.

By the way, since we're still playing in a swing rhythm, those three notes on beat four will be played as equally-spaced triplet notes.

Shuffle Riff Variation

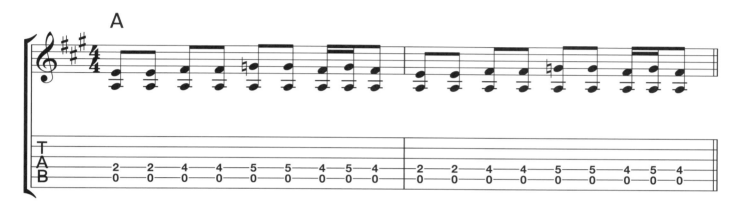

Okay, admit it—you really want to play lead guitar. You want to leap around the stage with your hands flailing across the fingerboard at breakneck speed! Well, it's going to take some time and work.

This book will give you some pointers—and get you started in the right direction.

We'll start by looking at some scales, as these are at the heart of lead playing, and we'll go on to explore some ways in which the notes from these scales can be used to build expressive solo phrases, called *licks*.

Minor Pentatonic Scales

Most rock guitar solos are based on minor pentatonic scales. Here's an E minor pentatonic scale:

Notice how it uses every open string?

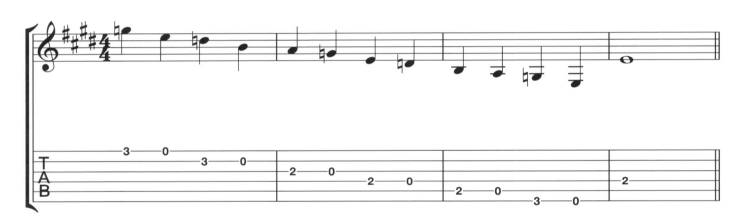

Here's a variation. It has an additional note, which creates a more bluesy sound. This extra note (the flattened fifth, as it's properly known) makes this scale an E blues scale:

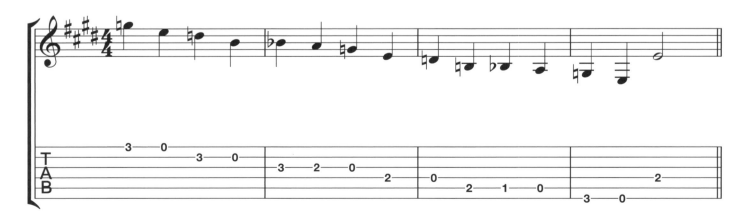

The blues scale is extremely versatile and expressive. As we'll see, it can be played elsewhere on the neck, allowing it to be adapted for any key.

Play these notes using your pick. For now, just use downward strokes. Later on, you'll want to go down and up to increase your speed. These bluesy notes are amazingly versatile. For example, if you're in the key of E, these notes will also sound fine with the A and B7 chords.

So, you can play through an entire blues in E using just a few notes!

As you progress, you'll learn to move these notes up the neck and into different keys. Stick with these examples until you can find the notes easily. Mastering the jump from the first string all the way down to the sixth string will take some serious practice. When you are familiar with the notes, try starting on the third string, or the fifth string, and create a little blues melody of your own. There are a lot of possibilities available to you using just a few notes...

Here's a simple lick to try using this E blues scale. There is a slide in the first bar, and it finishes off with a pair of pull-offs on the bottom two strings.

For the final two notes, tug the string a little with the left-hand finger as you pull it off, and you'll find the note bends in a blues style.

Often, it will make more sense to play some of these notes elsewhere on the neck. In the next example, the left hand operates between the 5th and 8th frets.

Place the 1st finger on the 5th fret, and assign the remaining fingers to one fret each—so the first notes are fretted with the 3rd finger.

Try to find different places to play the E blues scale. It will dramatically increase your knowledge of the guitar neck, as well as improving your left-hand technique.

BLUES SCALES IN OTHER KEYS

There are almost endless ways to plot scales on the guitar neck, and many guitarists dedicate years of practice to playing scales smoothly and confidently.

Moving the scale up three frets means you can play it in G instead. Notice that, whereas with the E blues scale every open string was used, the lowest fret this time is the third.

However, the simple shape that we looked at on page 36 can be placed elsewhere on the neck to create a blues scale in any key. Here are a few examples:

Focus on this third fret as an anchor point, keeping your 1st finger there. It'll mean you can find all the other notes without having to watch your hand position.

Likewise, up another two frets to the 5th it becomes an A blues scale.

At the 8th fret, it's now a C blues scale.

Finally, up at the 10th fret, we have a D blues scale.

OTHER POSITIONS

Returning to the E blues scale for a moment, it's worth mentioning that although it's very easy to play this scale right down at the bottom of the neck, making good use of all the open strings, there are plenty of other places in which to play the scale.

There are several reasons why you might want to do this: you might want to play in a different register (range); you might want to use a different tone, which can be achieved by playing certain notes on other strings: you might want to connect the scale to another scale; or you might want to use a particular chord shape to help orientate you on the neck.

Whatever the reason, it's worth having a look at some other places to play the scale. And, since these don't use open strings, they are very easily adapted to play the scale in different keys.

Incidentally, to make best use of the neck, don't feel you have to start or end the scale on E. Use the full range of the fretboard in your chosen position.

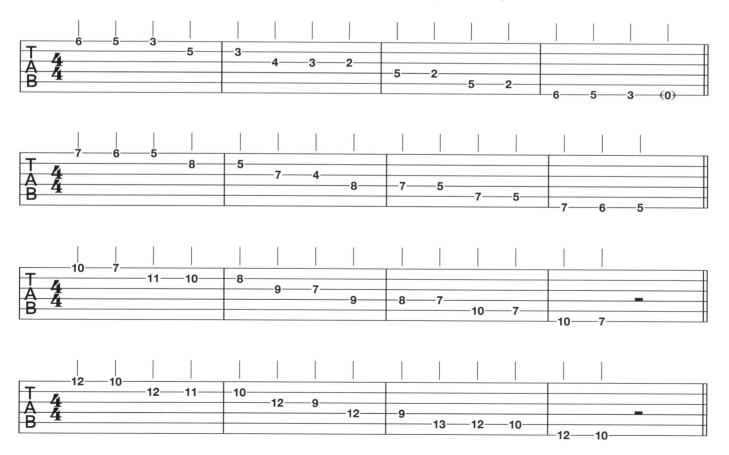

STRING BENDING

Most teachers won't even mention string bending until the student has made considerable progress with his or her playing. But you should be familiar with it from the very start.

As the blues moved north after World War II, blues players like B.B. King and Albert King figured out a way to get the slide sounds just by bending strings with their fingers.

String bending is an essential part of rock guitar playing, and every major rock guitarist, from Jimmy Page to Steve Vai, uses string-bending techniques in their riffs and solos.

Light strings make string bending easier, but it is still a difficult technique. Generally, strings are bent upward—raising the pitch. Let's try one on the third string. Place the 3rd finger of your left hand at the 7th fret of the third string. Play the third string with your pick. As the string rings out, push it towards you with your left hand. That's bending the string.

In the early days of country-blues guitar—from 1910 to 1945—many players used a bottleneck or a hollow piece of metal to get a sliding, shiny sound from their guitars. This technique is still used today. It is the trademark of such players as Bonnie Raitt, Johnny Winter, Ry Cooder, and Taj Mahal.

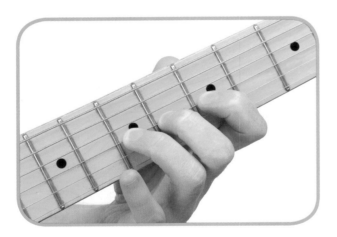

Now, there are many ways to bend a string and it may be years before you can do it properly. Still, keep this technique in mind as you continue your study of rock guitar. You might like to try it with the blues scale you've just learned. Pick the first string at the 3rd fret, and then push it upward as the string rings out. This should bend the string at a slightly higher pitch.

Some notes sound better bent than others, but don't be afraid to experiment!

Many guitarists like to use several fingers to give control to the bend.

Let's put this string bending technique into practice. Here are some rock licks in different keys that use the blues scale, with various bends built in.

The first lick, in E, has a series of bends up to B. The first, a whole tone bend, is held for a beat, then (still held as a pre-bend) it is played again.

Lastly, the held bend is played once more, and released to the natural 'unbent' note. Compare this lick with the one at the bottom of page 37, and hear what a difference the bends make.

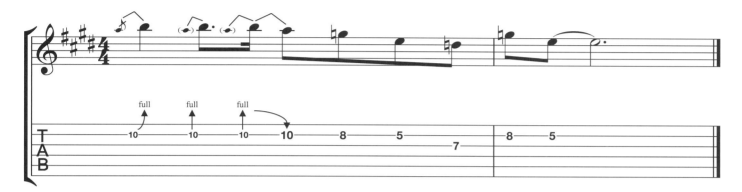

This one, in G, has a semitone bend in the first bar: pick at the normal pitch, then bend up. The following note is played on the same fret, so quickly release the bend before repicking. The bend in bar two is held up a whole tone—but with a vibrato on the sustained note.

Play this (as you hold the bend) by gently rocking the fretting finger back and forth across the fingerboard to create a subtly pulsating pitch change. The final bend is much like the first. Practise these techniques until you're able to create a vocal quality to the guitar sound.

Finally, a lick in A, beginning with a pre-bend: bend the string up a semitone before picking, and then release to the natural pitch.

In the second half of the lick, a slide and a bend are used to connect the flattened fifth to other notes of the scale.

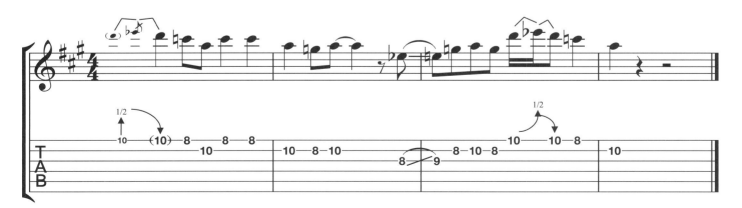

MAJOR PENTATONIC SCALES

The licks we've played so far come from the blues scale, which itself stems from a minor pentatonic scale (turn back to page 36 and take another look).

However, we've been using the blues scale in major keys, where we can expect the scale to clash with the chords we're likely to encounter.

Of course, that's not really a problem, because the dissonance caused by certain notes from the minor scale sounding against notes from major chords is a big part of what gives the blues scale its character, and is a big part of the sound of rock.

But equally, there is a scale that brings out the character of the major key rather than fighting against it. This is the *major pentatonic* scale.

Take another look at the E blues scale:

Here are the same notes rearranged, but this time played in the key of G:

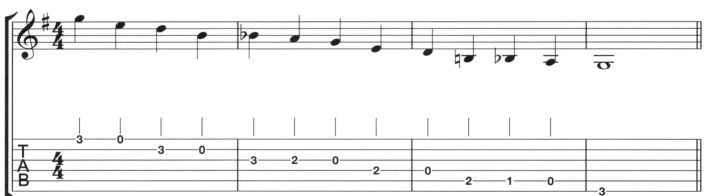

You can see that all the notes of the scale (with the exception of the B♭) are naturally occuring notes in the key of G. This means that you can use this scale in the key of G, too—and create a different sound.

Playing this scale in E makes a typically bluesy feel, but in G the effect is much less dark. Try these licks (opposite) to get an idea of the way the scale sounds used like this.

Play this lick with a light swing feel, and hear what might be termed a more 'wholesome' sound emerges. The dot above the final note in bar 2 is a *staccato* symbol, meaning the note should be played very short and detached.

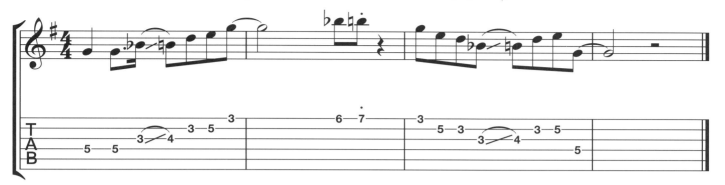

Now here's a rock 'n' roll-style phrase reminiscent of Chuck Berry. There are double stops (two notes on different strings fretted together with the same finger), and there's a bend in bar two. For the bend, fret the notes at the standard pitch, and gradually bend them up a semitone as the note continues. Try starting each slide with the 2nd finger on your left hand.

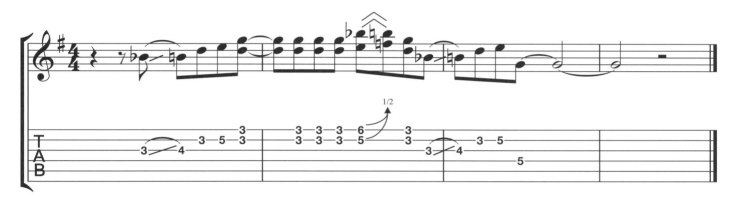

So what's happening here? We've used the same notes in the key of E and in the key of G to create two very different feels.

Well, the E blues scale ultimately originates from the scale of E minor; and the E minor scale uses the same notes as the G major scale. This G major scale is where the G major pentatonic scale comes from.

If you think of these notes as a palette that can either be applied to an E minor sound or a G major sound, you'll start to get an idea of their flexibility.

And finally: what happens if we combine the two feels? The next lick uses the G blues scales to begin, creating a gritty, tense sound. But at the end it uses notes from the G major pentatonic scale. which largely resolves that tension:

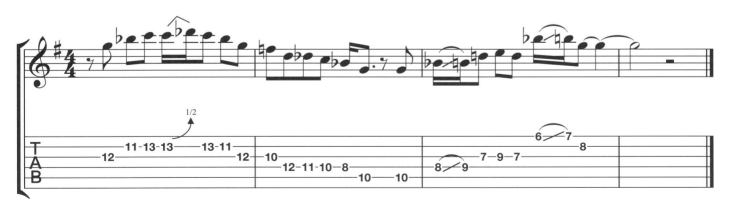

POWER CHORDS

Power chords are an essential part of a rock guitarist's arsenal. They're easy to learn, and they are incredibly versatile. So let's take a look.

They're also very simple. Try these examples (right):

These chords are neither major nor minor, since they don't have a third. In fact, they only contain the root and the fifth note of the chord, hence the '5' name.

It's the third that determines whether the chord is major or minor, and these shapes don't have one.

They also have a very distinctive sound. SInce there's no third, they sounds sparse, and lacking in harmonic colour.

These shapes have a lot going for them:

- They're really simple to play;

- They're versatile, since they *could* be played in place of either a minor or major chord;

- The E5 and A5 shapes are identical, except for the strings that are used, so there's even less to remember;

- They can easily be moved elsewhere on the neck to create other chords.

Historians often point to The Kinks—and in particular their song 'You Really Got Me'—as the first example of this type of chord in rock.

In fact, this shape was used in the blues long before. Pete Townshend of The Who coined the expression 'power chord'.

For all these reasons, this chord has found its way into the repertoire of guitarists, especially at the heavier end of the rock spectrum, where a powerful, overdriven, uncomplicated texture is often exactly what's called for.

Of course, playing up the neck with these shapes is simple, following the same system as that for bar chords (page 23).

Here are some examples of these shapes on starting on the 3rd fret. Use the 1st finger for the lowest note, and the 3rd and 4th fingers for the other two (below left):

In fact, many guitarists find it enough just to play the lowest two strings of the shape. This creates an even more sparse but powerful sound (below right):

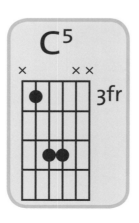

Power chords are often played in a very rhythmic, eighth-note strumming style. Try playing the following exercise using just downstrokes in a strong, even fashion.

Play an accented strum at the end of the first bar, tied on to the first beat of the second bar, so that the chord is sustained for a whole beat.

You'll notice that the chords stay on the bottom strings. You could move across to the fifth string for the A5 and C5 chords, but it's easier just to move up and down the neck.

Try this exercise at various speeds: slow and chugging, fast and furious... and if you have an distortion effect pedal, so much the better!

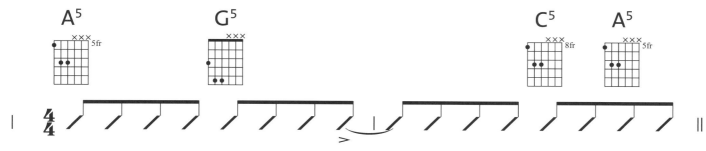

In the next exercise, you'll notice that the roots of the chords are taken from the E blues scale.

This is a great way to arrange power chords. Take the notes of a blues scale, and use them as a starting point for a selection of chords.

In this example, there are lots of off-beat accents. Try clapping the rhythm out until you're comfortable with it, and then strum it through. Take it slowly at first!

Some of these shapes are on the fifth string, and some on the sixth. Experiment with placing the chords.

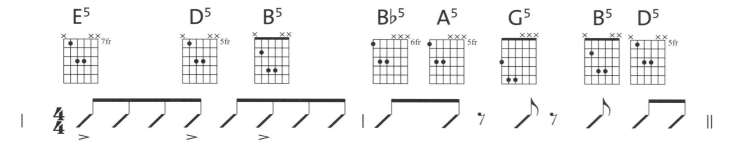

Once you start looking at songs in this style, you'll be amazed how far these simple power chord shapes will take you.

Try composing your own sequences using the chords in the exercise above. Once you have some phrases you like, record them as a backing track, and improvise over the top using the E blues scale.

You'll soon find certain licks will stick in the fingers and in the ears. Just add a solid drum beat and—hey presto—instant rock!

Take a look at page 48 to see more fully how to find these shapes on the guitar neck.

OTHER TUNINGS

Although the standard tuning is by far the most widespread, many rock bands acheive their sound by retuning the guitar. Here are a few of the most common variations:

Dropped D Tuning

One of the simplest of the alternative tunings, dropped D has the bottom string retuned a tone below standard tuning. This has various advantages: D chords can be played using all six strings—the bottom three all played open—creating a much richer texture (right); and power chords can be played using a simple bar across the bottom three strings (far right).

Dropped C Tuning

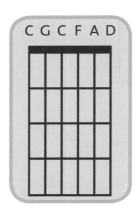

This is a variant of dropped D, with every string dropped a further tone. This produces a very heavy sound, which can almost be muddy due to the lack of tension in the strings. For this reason many guitarists switch to a heavier guage of strings.

Dropped C tuning has been used by Metallica and Ozzy Osbourne, and is favoured by many newer heavy metal bands such as System of a Down, P.O.D. and Papa Roach.

Check out System's *Toxicity* album for an effective example of dropped C tuning, making use of single-finger barred shapes on the bottom three strings.

Eb Tuning

Identical to standard tuning but with all six strings tuned down a semitone (one fret's-worth).

This tuning has been used by artists from Jimi Hendrix and Stevie Ray Vaughan, through Van Halen, Kiss and Motorhead to Nirvana and Guns N' Roses.

Tune the strings lower for a D or even C tuning.

Apart from the darker tone acheived with the lower range, many guitarists like the extra bend they can get on the strings due to the slacker tension, or alternatively being able to use a heavier gauge of strings.

If you're thinking of cultivating a 'detuned' sound, you might want to look at setting your guitar up with a nut that allows you to use heavier gauge strings—specifically with grooves that are wide and deep enough for thicker strings. If you're serious, you should even consider a separate guitar.

Open G Tuning

Bands from The Who, The Rolling Stones and Led Zeppelin to Pearl Jam have used open G, which has the distinct advantage of forming a chord with just the open strings—in this case G major.

This makes it ideal for slide guitar (listen to the Stones' *Wild Horses*) or for simple barring (right).

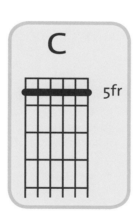

More Open Tunings

Several other open tunings can be used, of which the most popular is open D (left). Its minor equivalent is Dm tuning (near right).

Another useful variant is the open C tuning (far right). Of course, all open tunings are based on open chords, and can be retuned for different keys.

THE GUITAR NECK

Having a good understanding of the placement of notes on the neck gives the guitarist a huge advantage.

Not only can you locate scale patterns and licks in an instant, but you can use the bar chords and power chords we've looked at immediately too. Let's take a closer look at using those chord shapes.

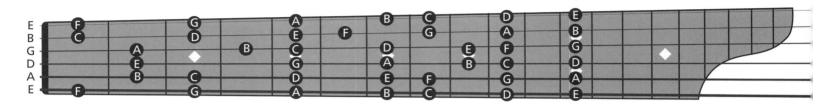

Looking at the strings of the guitar, you can see how the notes are positioned. Notice how there are two frets between almost all the pairs of letter names, but just *one* fret between B and C, and between E and F. To use power chords and bar chords fluently,

it's very useful to have a good idea of the placement of notes on the bottom two strings. Frets are counted from the nut up (left to right in this diagram). Notice how, at the 12th fret, the open string note names are repeated.

Finding Bar Chords

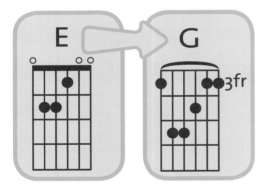

Bar chords (page 23) use two types of shapes: E-type and A-type.

For E-type chords, find the fret you're after by looking along the sixth string. For example, if you want to play G, play an E shape barred on the 3rd fret—since there's a G on the 3rd fret of the sixth string (left).

For A-type chords, simply look along the fifth string. If you want to play D7, use an A7 shape barred on the 5th fret, as that's where there's a D (right).

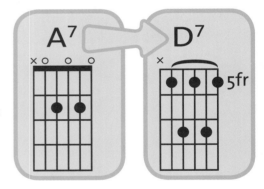

Finding Power Chords

Power chords (pages 44-45) are very simple to use. Move the shape up on either the E string or A string until it's on the note that the chord is named after.

For example, to play D5, place it either on the 10th fret of the bottom E string, or on the 5th fret of the A string (left).

If you wanted to play F5, place the shape at the 1st fret of the bottom string, or on the 8th fret of the fifth string (right).

1 2 3 4 5 6 7 8 9